To

From

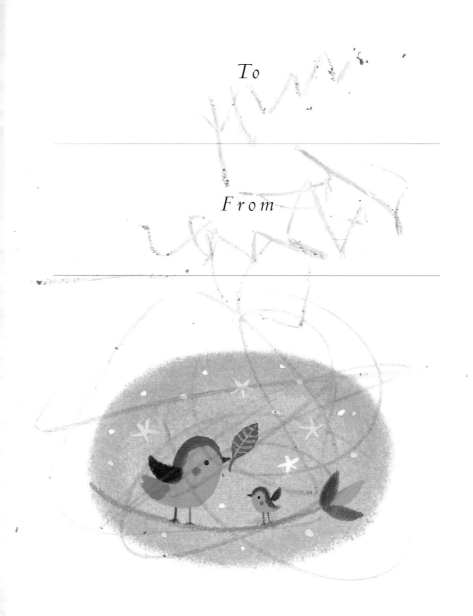

Written and compiled by Elena Pasquali
Illustrations copyright © 2013 Dubravka
Kolanovic
This edition copyright © 2013 Lion
Hudson

Published by Lion Children's Books
an imprint of
Lion Hudson plc
Wilkinson House, Jordan Hill Road,
Oxford OX2 8DR, England
www.lionhudson.com/lionchildrens

ISBN 978 0 7459 6378 5

First edition 2013

Acknowledgments

Every effort has been made to trace and
contact copyright owners for material
used in this book. We apologize for any
inadvertent omissions or errors.

All unattributed prayers are by Elena
Pasquali and Lois Rock, copyright ©
Lion Hudson. Prayers by Sophie Piper,
Christina Goodings, and Mary Joslin are
copyright © Lion Hudson.

A catalogue record for this book is
available from the British Library

Printed and bound in China, January
2013, LH17

Safe this Night

Elena Pasquali * Dubravka Kolanovic

LION
CHILDREN'S

Good night! Good night!
Far flies the light;
But still God's love
Shall shine above,
Making all bright,
Good night! Good night!

Victor Hugo (1802–85)

Contents

Day is done

Day is done,
Gone the sun
From the lake,
From the hills,
From the sky.
Safely rest,
All is well!
God is nigh.

Anonymous

Who made the night-time shadows?
Who made each silver star?
Who made the moon that floats on high
Where clouds and angels are?

The One who made the morning sun,
The daytime sky of blue,
The One who made both you and me
And loves both me and you.

Sophie Piper

Blackbird sings a goodnight prayer
Rabbit sniffs the evening air
Moon shines down from heaven above
I am safe in God's great love.

God has counted the stars in the heavens,
God has counted the leaves on the tree;
God has counted the children on earth:
I know God has counted me.

13

God, who made the earth,
The air, the sky, the sea,
Who gave the light its birth,
Careth for me.

God, who made the grass,
The flower, the fruit, the tree,
The day and night to pass,
Careth for me.

God, who made all things,
On earth, in air, in sea,
Who changing seasons brings,
Careth for me.

Sarah Betts Rhodes (1824–1904)

May God clothe me,
may God feed me;
may God guide me,
may God lead me;
may God comfort
and defend me,
with encircling love
befriend me.

Mary Joslin

The darkness comes:
Give thanks for the night.

The stars appear:
Give thanks for their light.

The air is still:
Give thanks for the calm.

And God is here:
Keep us safe from harm.

Sophie Piper

20

Time for bed

Thank you, dear God, for the little
place that is my home – more special
to me than all the stars in the universe.

Bless the window
Bless the door
Bless the ceiling
Bless the floor
Bless this place which is our home
Bless us as we go and come.

The circle of my family,
the circle of my friends
are safe within the circle
of the love that never ends.

Sophie Piper

At the ending of the day
Troubles must be put away
Quarrels must be laid to rest
So that we at peace may rest.

Sunrise and sunset
are like you and me:
though we are quite different
we both can agree
that there is one daytime
and there is one night
and God's golden sunshine
to give us all light.

26

Shadows in the hallway
Shadows on the stair
God be always near me
God be everywhere.

Guard us through the night, dear God,
and keep us safe from harm;
from all our wild imaginings
and every false alarm.

God bless you in the dark hours,
God bless you through the night,
God bless you, little baby,
For ever in God's sight.

God bless you, little baby,
Whose life has just begun,
God keep you safe, so you may find
Your own place in the sun.

Sophie Piper

Dear God, bless all my family,
as I tell you each name;
and please bless each one differently
for no one's quite the same.

God bless all those that I love;
God bless all those that love me;
God bless all those that love those
that I love,
And all those that love those that love me.

From an old New England sampler

Lord, send me sleep that I may live;
The wrongs I've done this day forgive.
Bless every deed and thought and word
I've rightly done, or said, or heard.
Bless relatives and friends alway;
Teach all the world to watch and pray.
My thanks for all my blessings take
And hear my prayer for Jesus' sake.

Author unknown

God in heaven, hear my prayer,
Keep me in thy loving care.
Be my guide in all I do,
Bless all those who love me too.

Traditional

Now I lay me down to sleep,
I pray thee, Lord, thy child to keep;
Thy love to guard me through the night
And wake me in the morning light.

Traditional

I go to sleep upon my bed,
The bat hangs down his sleepy head,
The mouse curls up into a ball
While God is watching over all.

Sophie Piper

36

Safe this night

Lord, keep us safe this night,
Secure from all our fears;
May angels guard us while we sleep,
Till morning light appears.

John Leland (1754—1841)

I see the moon
And the moon sees me;
God bless the moon
And God bless me.

Traditional

39

God bless the night-time creatures
in the shadows of the wood;
may they live their secret lives
as wild creatures should.

May they find their secret paths
through all the moonlit dark;
may they find their secret homes
when morning wakes the lark.

The moon is afloat
on the heavenly sea
and I wait on dreamland's shore;
dear God, let me sleep
through the dark so deep
until the night is no more.

Clouds in the sky above,
Waves on the sea,
Angels up in heaven
Watching over you and me.

Christina Goodings

Deep peace of the running waves to you,
Deep peace of the flowing air to you,
Deep peace of the quiet earth to you,
Deep peace of the shining stars to you,
Deep peace of the shades of night to you,
Moon and stars always giving light to you,
Deep peace of Christ, the son of Peace,
to you.

Traditional Gaelic blessing

The moon shines bright,
The stars give light
Before the break of day;
God bless you all
Both great and small
And send a joyful day.

Traditional

Now the night is over
Day is drawing near
Shade me from the sunshine
Drive away all fear.

Save me from the dangers
Of the clear blue day
God, while I lie sleeping,
Ever with me stay.

Prayer of the Owl

A new day

Thank you, God in heaven,
For a day begun.
Thank you for the breezes,
Thank you for the sun.
For this time of gladness,
For our work and play,
Thank you, God in heaven,
For another day.

Traditional

A little seed
unfolds its leaves
and grows up to the light;
and I will lift
my face to heaven
and learn to do what's right.

Morning is dawning
creation awakening
the birds and the flowers and me
we look to the sun
and we reach for the sky
to grow into all we should be.

Baby creatures, just awakened,
You are part of God's creation;
Baby creatures, oh, so small,
God is father of us all.

Open my eyes
so I can see
the ways I could
more useful be.

Give me the strength
and heart and mind
to do the things
that are good and kind.

Sophie Piper

Little deeds of kindness,
Little words of love,
Help to make earth happy,
Like the heaven above.

Julia Carney (1823–1908)

Let my life shine
like a star in the night,
filling my world
with goodness and light.

For blessings here
and those in store
we give thanks now
and evermore.

Index of first lines

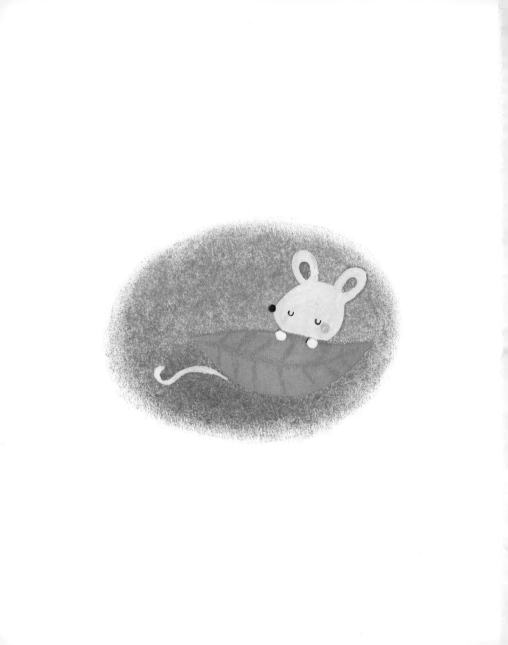